The Glory of Gold

The Glory of Gold

A contemporary approach to gilding

SUE TRYTELL

SALLY MILNER PUBLISHING

*I dedicate this book to opportunity and thrift
shops all over the world for providing
an endless supply of other people's trash
that is my treasure.
There is always a new beginning –
there is no end.*

S U E   T R Y T E L L

For my Father

First published in 1995 by
Sally Milner Publishing Pty Ltd
558 Darling Street
Rozelle NSW 2039 Australia

© Sue Trytell 1995

National Library of Australia
Cataloguing-in-Publication data:

Trytell, Sue
    The glory of gold

    ISBN 1 86351 146 6

    1. Gilding-Amateurs' manuals. 2. Gilding-Technique.
    I. Title (Series: Milner craft series).

745.75

Design and typesetting by Sandra Horth
Photography by Neil Lorimer
Styling by Jane Devine and Sue Trytell
Colour separation in Hong Kong by
Wellmak Printing Press Ltd
Printed in Australia by Impact Printing

Acknowledgements

This project has been made possible – and exciting – by the help and

devotion of a band of people. Without their assistance I could not have

achieved my goals.

My thanks go to the following.

- THE WEYERMANN FAMILY for their trust and faith in my work and for the use of their products. Their co-operation and generous provision of all gilding supplies and leaf enabled me to gild almost everything in sight – and more.

- HEATHER RUSSELL, my text writer, who with enthusiasm and exuberance was always ready to translate my visuals into words.

- NEIL LORIMER, photographer, for splendid detail, artistic style and creative reflection. Without this, the merit of my work would be greatly diminished. The pieces shine through his lens.

- LISA DONATH, my other pair of hands, who excitedly carried out every task set. Her invaluable help allowed me to explore yet another opportunity shop for more surfaces to work on.

- JANE DEVINE, artist and friend, who encouraged, created works and cared enough to always be there when called upon and whose superb eye for detail always showed me another perspective.

- GRAHAM RICE FLOWERS, Toorak, for generously supplying the blooms used in the photography.

- KIM HARPER of Harper and Sandilands for Porter's Paints, eighteenth-century reproduction paper and lamp shade.

- JUNE WILHELM of Romantique Haberdashery for the props and project pieces used throughout the book.

- MINIATURE WORLD AND CRAFT, for the doll's house accessories used to make bottle stoppers.

- PIONEER CRAFT for sponsoring Deco Art Ultra Gloss Enamel Paints.

- INTERGRAIN, for sponsoring products for use on a variety of surfaces.

- TERRACOTTA ETC for all the terracotta pieces.

- TRISH HARPER, GAYE JACKSON, SALLY LUCK, ROC ART, FAY SCOTT, BETTYE KAMEVAAR AND KATE SELLARS JONES, for contributing special projects from their artistic worlds.

- JENNIFER GILBERT, BARBARA ROBB AND SALLY MILNER PUBLISHING for believing in my work, and my husband, BRAHAM, for constantly putting up with all my 'stuff'.

Contents

*A country
provincial touch.*

Introduction

*G*old is the universal prize
in all countries, in all
cultures, in all ages...
*gold for greed, gold for splendour,
gold for adornment, gold for
reverence, gold for power,
sacrificial gold, life-giving gold,
gold for tenderness, barbaric gold,
voluptuous gold...*

(*from* The Ascent of Man *by J. Bronowski*)

The power of gold

The quest for gold has played a huge part in the shaping of the world's history. Gold represents a coming together of spirituality, science, artistry, philosophy and the many conflicting emotions of greed, lust, vanity, power and love. Gold is woven into the fabric of both extraordinary and ordinary people's lives all over the world.

There are ancient legends of greed, like the story of Midas, a legendary Phrygian king who earned the favour of the god Dionysius. Dionysius asked him to make a wish whereupon Midas asked that everything he touched turn to gold. His wish was granted, but much to his horror he found that his food and drink turned to gold. Luckily Dionysius took pity on him and sent him to bathe in the river.

The invasion of Peru by the Spaniards in 1532 is probably the most tragic story of greed. When Atahualpa, the Inca ruler, was held captive by the Spanish conquistador, Francisco Pizarro, he offered the Spaniards a mighty ransom of gold in return for his life. Even though Atahualpa fulfilled his side of the bargain, filling a room nearly three metres high with gold, Pizarro double crossed him. The betrayed Inca king lost his life, his gold and ultimately his kingdom.

The Incas worshipped the sun. The brilliance and radiance of gold resembled the sun's own radiance, so Inca temples, as well as containing extraordinary gold artefacts such as masks, statues, pitchers, vases etc., had walls lined with gold, particularly on the side where the sun rose. The ransacking of Cuzco by the conquistadors is said to be one of the rarest moments in history when the capital of a great empire was pillaged at will: an invasion of greed. The beautiful Inca treasures and cultural artefacts were melted down, representing a tragic artistic and cultural loss. Soon after the ransacking, news of gold spread like wildfire, and Spaniards stampeded particularly from the Caribbean settlements, to the wilds of Peru in search of their fortunes.

Gold has continued to grip the imagination and passion of ordinary people. The gold rush phenomenon,

and the search for gold has dominated much Australian history. Gold was discovered at Ballarat in August 1851, and within three months Ballarat's population had risen to 10 000, and trebled a year later. Within three years, Victoria's population had trebled, and during that decade alone 33 new towns were established on the Victorian gold fields as a result of the peculiar disease known as gold fever.

What is it about gold that inspires such ruthlessness, greed and such passion? Is there more to man's lust for gold than just its monetary value and scarcity? Ancient alchemists didn't value gold for its scarcity and monetary value, they valued gold because it was incorruptible. To the alchemists, gold was the symbol of immortality; gold represented the sun. These qualities related to the physical properties of gold which allow it to be melted down time and time again without spoiling. Gold resists chemical attack and is not corroded by air. Its low melting point and malleability mean that it can be worked and beaten paper thin (up to 0.0001 mm), so thin that it can be used to adorn, encase or cover an object, giving it the appearance of solid gold. These unique properties inspired alchemists to search for the elixir of life: to make gold out of base chemicals, thus achieving immortality. Gold is, on the one hand, the most precious and most expensive

A gaming table.

of metals, revered and used to impress by kings, queens, rulers and spiritual leaders all over the world. On the other hand, it plays a special part in the lives of ordinary people. Gold is a traditional gift on special occasions, such as weddings and Golden Wedding anniversaries (the fiftieth anniversary of marriage). Gold jewellery, watches, rings and brooches are treasured by families and inherited by their children, forming a material connection, the cultural heritage of one generation passed on to the next. In India, a special food called Varca is gilded with 22 carat gold and eaten on special occasions and there is a European liqueur called Gold Wasser, containing tiny fragments of genuine 22 carat gold.

It is this fascination and lure of gold by people of all cultures which makes gilding such an irresistible art form. In the Americas, knowledge of metal technology was most advanced in Peru. Use of beaten gold leaf can be dated back to 2000 BC in the Andes of Southern Peru. Well before this though, the ancient Egyptians were able to cast gold to make small statues and jewellery. They also had the ability to work large masses of gold, as is shown by the gold coffin of Tutankhamun in Cairo, which weighs more than 300 lbs. Egyptian craftsmen beat gold into fine sheets by laying the gold on a flat stone then beating it with another stone. Gold leaf was freely used to gild statues, mummy masks, coffins and other items of funerary equipment.

In Europe, gilding was used extensively in the Renaissance, Baroque and Rococo periods to adorn furniture such as tables, picture frames, chairs and mirror frames. Icons, picture frames and art work

heavily gilded with genuine gold still adorn temples and places of worship all over the world.

There have been few changes in the process of beating gold over the last four hundred years. Gold ingots are rolled into a continuous paper-thin ribbon. Until the early part of this century, all gold leaf was then beaten by hand, and some of it still is. In the 1920s, a machine was invented which could reproduce the action of a hand-wielded hammer, and more recent developments have seen gold being beaten between sheets of plastic, instead of between the traditional fine skin of ox-gut known as gold-beater's skin.

Knowledge of the art of gilding enables everyday objects to be transformed so that they glow with the warmth and richness of gold. These objects are immediately accessible, part of everyday life. Gilding favourite objects, broken down treasures, or bits of junk offers the opportunity to experiment with a material that is usually perceived to be quite out of reach. Playing with gold may sound a bit decadent, but if used judiciously and tastefully gilding can create a beautiful *objet d'art*, or an unusual individual effect.

My own earliest memories of gold were in museums, places of worship and in architectural detail. I remember being entranced by the glow of gilded picture frames, icons and church decorations. I loved being in these places, watching the sun play on the gold. Knowing as I do now, the place of gold in the history of so many different cultures and peoples, I like to feel that my work expresses a delicate balance between cultures, past and

present. My art encompasses an awareness of my cultural and geographical position in the world.

Transformations

In the objects I select for gilding, I am looking for images that trigger my imagination and unlock memories of family and social history. Objects carry with them all sorts of cultural memories, and to this end I am most grateful to the opportunity shops and thrift shops of this world for storing other people's treasures from other times, other eras – treasures that add to my file of preserved memory. These 'op' shops have enabled me to put this book together. Being a bower bird, my joy is to collect 'stuff' and then transform it – giving it a new lease of life.

The old adage 'beauty is in the eye of the beholder' or 'one person's trash is

'Be my Valentine'. From ceramic to food, paper and beyond.

Bringing in the sun.

another person's treasure' to me has rung true many times. Good design no matter what the era will hold steadfast. It may lose its lustre, but with a little help can be reclaimed as a piece of beauty. There are always new beginnings. Of course, some pieces are so beautiful it is wise to leave them alone: 'better less than more'.

My feelings, imagination and ideas to create are also stimulated by nature. Always striving to widen my creative horizon, the natural world holds endless inspiration. Watching the tide come in washing up objects from the sea floor has an irresistible magic about it. Kelp, shells and then, behold, a small old bottle gleaming magically in the sun, empty of contents but full of sea stories untold.

It is for re-use as contained, or container, possibly my message implanted in and around it.

The natural environment is a window that frames my world of transformations, and provides an assemblage of materials for adornment. My art, driven by a concern about the destruction of the natural environment, is dedicated to the world's lost habitats, horizons or endangered places.

My message – transform the ordinary. Everyday objects carry stories and memories. Don't discard them – transform them and let them adorn your life!

how to use this book

This book is intended to be a source of ideas and inspiration, a guide to any novice craft gilder and a wide range of people who wish to use this medium simply, easily and effectively. I hope all beginners feel confident in their use of this book.

As practice and the use of various materials will change your approach to each piece, search the photographs for clues on how the leaf has been used.

Don't be tempted to use gold paint instead of leaf. It cannot produce the same sheen, lustre and effect as leaf. The sun shining down on a gilded spade handle in the garden (even an old one) makes it easily identifiable. Try it ... and you'll be hooked too.

Look at different cultures, eras, centuries. Examine patterning, motifs on paper, patterns in embroidery, fabric, even pavements, e.g. look at the effect of water on an oil patch on a road. It resembles the colours and patterns of variegated metal leaf. Designs in nature are rarely wrong. Study the patterns on animals, birds, fish. These are tokens before your eyes. Use them. When days are overcast and seem dull, bring in the sun. Gild a piece or two.

happy playing

Materials & Tools

Here is a brief description of all the materials and tools needed to prepare, gild and finish pieces similar to those photographed throughout the book. The basic requirements for each surface are given at the beginning of every workshop. Included in the list below are some technical terms, such as tamp and skewings, used in the gilding process.

The gilding method described in this book does not require traditional gilder's tools, such as a gilder's tip, gilder's cushion, gilder's knife or burnishing stone. Instead, everyday art and craft tools, such as paint brushes, scissors and foam applicators, as well as simple home-made tools like a car sponge and a bob are used. More importantly, all the materials used in this method are water-based, non-toxic and environmentally friendly. Instead of the traditional bole base-coat and signwriter's size, this method uses gilding milk – a water-based, non-toxic adhesive – and acrylic paints, sealers and shellac as base coats.

Apart from the leaf, gilding milk, and some specialist finishes like rotten-stone, which are only available from gilding suppliers, most of the materials and tools are readily available from art and craft suppliers, paint shops and the craft section in major department stores.

Asphaltum – Liquid asphalt created by mixing bituminous black paint with turpentine. It is used to achieve a tortoiseshell look over the leaf.

Backing paper –Tissue or wax paper on which the leaf is mounted for easier handling.

Base coat – Shellac, paint, gesso or a sealer applied mainly to porous surfaces, before the gilding milk and leaf is applied.

Beeswax – Furniture polish, which can be buffed with a soft rag. It is used to create clear sheen over the leaf.

Bituminous black – Black paint mixed with turpentine to create liquid asphalt or asphaltum. Available from paint shops.

Bleach – This is used to kill any bacteria growing on concrete or other old surfaces.

Bob – A home-made tool made of cotton wadding wrapped in muslin, calico or silk and tied with a rubber band.

Brushes – These are used to apply the base and final coats, to tamp leaf down and to apply finishes. Bristle, ox hair, sable, and even cosmetic brushes, are some of the extensive range of brushes used in the gilding process. The range and quality of brushes used are important as unsuitable brushes can result in the surface not being as you would want. Brushes should be thoroughly washed in warm soapy water and carefully stored as soon after use as possible.

Calico – This is washed and dried to make a bob.

Cotton rags – These are used for applying the finishing cream.

Crackle medium – A substance that produces cracks in the painted surface to give it an aged or weathered look. It is water-based, non-toxic and available from art and craft suppliers and paint shops.

A selection of tools and materials for use throughout this book.

Craft knife – A variety of craft knives are available with replaceable blades. They are used for cutting stencils and the gold leaf.

Cutting mat – a self-healing mat is best.

Decadry – Dry transfer lettering. See Letraset.

Decals – Two dimensional transfers for decorating a piece after it has been gilded. These are available from art and craft suppliers. (See page 80 for Suppliers and Distributors.)

Distemper (Porter's) – A traditional paint for interior use only, made by binding powdered chalk, organic animal glue and powders. It dries to a soft, velvety texture, which is dead flat and chalky. The unusual opacity and depth of distemper colours are quite distinctive. Available from paint shops.

Double-sided adhesive tape – This is used for gilded bands, strips or small cut-out designs.

Foam applicator – A foam brush used to apply gesso, paint or sealer. It will minimise brush strokes. Available from art and craft suppliers and paint shops in a variety of sizes.

Gilding cream – A finishing cream used over the leaf. Treasure Gold, Talens Pate, Gold Finger, Antique Paste and Liberon are just some of the brand names of gilding creams available in Australia. Gilding cream is available in a wide range of colours and can be obtained from art and craft suppliers or gilding suppliers.

Gilding milk – A non-toxic, white (which is why it is called milk), latex-based adhesive that is applied directly under the leaf. Gilding milk is a European product, similar to quicksize. (See page 80 for Suppliers and Distributors.)

Gloves – You will need latex gloves to protect your hands when applying shellac and gilding milk, and cotton gloves to wear when applying leaf, to stop it from sticking to your fingers and to avoid fingerprints tarnishing the leaf.

Glue – Assorted glues may be required for attaching decorations and repairing broken objects.

Gesso – A white primer used for priming surfaces such as wood and bisque-fired ceramics. Gesso is a bonding coat that can be sanded back to a very smooth finish. Available from art and craft suppliers.

Gold leaf – This is available in 12-24 carat. It can be bought mounted on backing paper or in loose sheets, in books of 25 sheets. Each sheet is 80 x 80 mm. (See page 80 for Suppliers and Distributors.)

Letraset – Dry-transfer lettering that can be used as a decorative effect over leaf. Lettering comes in a variety of colours and is available from newsagents and art and craft suppliers.

Masking tape – Self-adhesive paper tape that is easily removed, used for masking out areas to be gilded, providing a clean edge and holding down stencils.

Metal leaf – This includes Dutch metal (imitation gold), aluminium leaf, copper leaf and variegated leaf. The variegated leaf is available in a range of colours, including red gold, blue gold, green gold and various autumn tints. Metal leaf is sold mounted on layers of backing paper or in loose sheets, in books of 25 sheets. Each leaf is 140 x140 mm. Aluminium and copper leaf is also available in this format. (See page 80 for Suppliers and Distributors.)

Methylated spirits – Used for adding to shellac flakes and for surface cleaning.

Modelling paste – A white paste used to create a rough surface underneath

the leaf. Available from art and craft suppliers. Also known as texture paste.

Paint – Artist's oils or acrylic paints are used at various stages of the gilding process. Acrylic house paint can also be used. Deco Art Ultra Gloss acrylic enamel (Pioneer Craft) can be used to paint designs over the leaf.

Paper – This is used to cover work surface when applying leaf. Use a large sheet of heavy, white paper.

Plastic cloth – Used to cover the work surface during application of base coats

and gilding milk. Use a heavy plastic film, old plasticised table cloth, or even old X-ray film.

Rottenstone – Powdered limestone is used as a finish after gilding to achieve an aged, dusty effect. Available from gilding suppliers.

Sandpaper – Required for preparing and cleaning surfaces. Use 60-1200-grit wet-and-dry for very fine sanding.

Scalpel – Needed for cutting the leaf.

Scissors – Sharp scissors are used for cutting the leaf.

Schlag metal – See metal leaf.

Sealer – Use a clear sealer or clear varnish, such as Wattyl Speed Clear, Liquitex, Jo Sonja, Intergrain Ultraclear, Matisse. Available in matt, satin or gloss finishes. This is applied over the leaf to protect it and prevent it from wearing off and tarnishing. Sometimes also used as a base coat or added as a medium to paint for increased strength. Available from art and craft suppliers and paint shops.

Shellac – This is used as a base or final coat. Known as 'French furniture polish' or as a resin varnish, it can be bought from large paint or hardware shops in bags of flakes and made into solution by adding methylated spirits, or it can be bought pre-mixed. Use it as a final coat to protect the leaf from tarnishing and wearing off.

Shoe polish – Can be used as a finishing cream over leaf to subdue the brightness. Use a cream shoe polish not a liquid, and preferably choose one with its own foam applicator, such as Padawax.

Silver leaf – Genuine silver leaf is available mounted on backing paper or in loose sheets, in books of 25 sheets. Each sheet is 95 x 95 mm.

Skewings – Fragments of leaf rubbed off during the gilding process. These are saved in a box or jar for patching gaps and fractures in the leaf or gilding small pieces.

Sponge – Have a synthetic car sponge to apply gilding milk and a natural sea sponge to apply asphaltum or paint.

Spray bottle – This is used to apply asphaltum.

Steel wool – 000 to 0000 grades, used to distress leaf.

Stencils – An ancient way to create repeating patterns. Stencils can be made from various materials such as stencil paper, acetate or mylar.

Stains and dyes – These are used as a base coat, particularly on wood or blown eggs.

Stippling – A painting technique where the paint is dabbed on the surface in irregular patterns or drifts, creating a fur-like appearance.

Tack cloth – A cloth used for removing dust from surfaces before gilding.

Tamp – Running a brush over a gilded surface to ensure that the leaf has adhered. This process also removes skewings.

Texture paste – See modelling paste.

Turpentine – This is mixed with bituminous black to create asphaltum.

Tweezers – Useful for picking up skewings and decals.

Varnish – This is applied over the metal leaf on some surfaces to prevent wearing and tarnishing. Use a water-based, matt, semi-matt, satin or full gloss finish. Readily available from paint and hardware shops.

Woodfiller – Use this for filling holes in wooden surfaces.

The children's story, from miniature doll's house accessories to the lid of a lolly jar.

The Basics

Before embarking on any gilding project, there are questions that must always be considered to decide how the piece should be transformed.

• Should the piece be evenly gilded, or have a fractured, aged look?
• Does the piece need to be gilded all over or is just a touch of leaf sufficient (for example, bands of leaf or a gilded, stencilled design), or should selected areas only be gilded, such as the handles of a tray?
• Should the piece be further enhanced with decorations, either gilded or ungilded?
• Should the piece to be gilded so it is bright and eye-catching or should it be deceptively delicate?

Naturally, there are no right or wrong answers to these questions. However, the gilded pieces photographed in this book are there to give you ideas and inspiration, examples of different styles and possible effects that can be achieved using the materials listed in the previous chapter and the techniques outlined in this chapter. These photographs are my way of helping you answer these artistic questions for yourself, to achieve the desired look for your particular piece. Photographs can speak a thousand words, so study them closely before you embark on a project. Find out what you like and what you don't like. Having said that, my other piece of advice is: be playful, don't be afraid to experiment. As long as you don't compromise on good design and shape in the first instance (that is, in your choice of piece), there are always ways of changing or covering up mistakes in the gilding. And in the meantime, you might create something precious, something unusual, something bold. Above all else, enjoy yourself.

Before we begin, there is just one other thing to bear in mind. This book describes how to gild decorative and functional household objects. While some objects you may gild, like the handles of stainless steel cutlery or ceramic underplates, can be functional, they cannot be treated as you would treat gold-plated cutlery or fired ceramics. The gilding treatment described here is not as robust or permanent as gold plating. The objects you gild must be handled and cleaned carefully.

There are six basic steps in gilding. They are as follows.

A blue base-painted frame with imitation gold leaf and gold gilding surrounding winter poppies.

STEP 1: Preparation of the surface
STEP 2: Base coat
STEP 3: Applying gilding milk
STEP 4: Applying the leaf
STEP 5: Finishes and decorative effects
STEP 6: The final coat

STEP 1: *PREPARATION OF SURFACE*

Thorough cleaning is a must for all pieces. Clean with warm, soapy water, using stronger agents such as methylated spirits or vinegar and water if necessary. Bleach the object if bacteria are present. Once the piece is clean, any further preparation entirely depends on the final look you are trying to achieve. Consider whether you want a smooth, even look or a look that incorporates the imperfections of the piece. Scrape, clean, fill, repair, sand or remove unwanted bits accordingly. The only other issue is surface decoration. If you are going to gild over the top of a decoration like a shell or moulding, glue it on at this stage using a glue appropriate to the surface and the object.

STEP 2: *BASE COAT*

Before applying gold leaf to a piece you must first consider whether it needs an application of a base coat to seal the original surface. If the surface is a sealed, non-porous surface such as glass, plastic, stainless steel or porcelain, there is no need to apply a base coat as the gilding milk will sit evenly on the sealed surface and provide a good, tacky medium for the leaf to adhere to. If the surface is porous, for example, wood, raw metal, terracotta, bisque-fired ceramics or paper, gilding milk will be absorbed into the surface. In these instances the surface must be sealed first before the gilding milk and leaf are applied. Base coats of shellac, gesso, paint or sealer are used depending on the surface and the desired effect. Stains and dyes are also acceptable base coats and are particularly effective on wood and eggs. One or two coats of a base coat can be applied depending on the porosity of the surface. If in doubt, apply two coats.

Your choice of base coat depends on the porosity of the surface and the effect you are aiming to achieve. If you want a base coat colour to show through the leaf, use a coloured paint. I sometimes add sealer to paint for added strength. If no base coat colour is desired, use shellac. On wood where a smooth surface is required, gesso is used as it can be sanded to a very smooth finish. Different base coats can be used in conjunction; for example, a coat of gesso followed by shellac, or gesso followed by paint.

Shellac

Shellac is known in Australia as 'French furniture polish'. It can be bought from large paint or hardware shops in bags of flakes and is made into solution by adding methylated spirits. It can also be purchased pre-mixed in the form of traditional white polish, blonde, de-waxed shellac. This is particularly good as a base coat for paper.

Shellac is a sealer that can, where necessary, be applied underneath and on top of leaf. Underneath, it provides a protective surface that isolates the leaf from the base surface. This is particularly important when working with a metal leaf such as Dutch metal or variegated leaf because this may tarnish on contact with some base surfaces. Applying leaf between two coats of shellac provides a completely sealed unit, which minimises the possibility of tarnishing. This means that for some sealed non-porous surfaces, such as stainless steel and plastic, where no base coat is required for the leaf to adhere properly, you may choose to apply a coat of shellac to minimise tarnishing. However, in my experience, as long as cotton gloves are worn and the leaf is well sealed over the top, preventing any contact with the air, tarnishing is generally not a problem.

Serviette rings gilded in a variety of metal leaf. Left to right: wood, metal, plastic buttons and plastic.

Preparation

1. Make up the shellac solution in a jar with a tightly fitting lid. Two thirds fill a clean dry glass jar with the shellac flakes. Add enough methylated spirits to cover the flakes. Stir well. Different coloured shellacs take different lengths of time to dissolve. For example, button and ruby are harder pieces and take days to dissolve. Stir frequently. Once dissolved, shellac can be stored for future use.

2. Make a bob to apply the shellac. Use a 10 cm square of natural soft fabric, such as washed muslin, washed calico or silk, and a small wad of kapok or cotton wadding about the size of a ping-pong ball. Don't use cotton wool as it will soak up too much liquid. The wadding can be bought from upholsterers' suppliers or large craft suppliers. Wrap the muslin around the kapok and secure it with a small rubber band. A bob will only last for one work session, because once dry it becomes too hard and must be thrown out. If applying shellac to a large surface or a number of pieces, add another swatch of fabric over the bob with another elastic band if the first one wears out. Alternatively, make plenty of bobs before starting the project.

3. Wear latex gloves when applying the shellac and cover your work surface with a heavy sheet of plastic or an old plasticised table cloth.

Application

1. Stir the shellac solution well and tip a small amount into a smaller container. Don't work from the storage jar. Dip about half of the end of the bob into the shellac solution. Don't saturate the bob completely.

2. Wipe the wet bob over the piece using firm, even strokes, preferably working in one direction. Only wipe the area once.

3. Apply shellac to all areas of the piece that are to be gilded.

4. Leave to dry (it dries quickly, within 20 minutes).

5. Repeat if you feel the surface is not adequately sealed. Paper, for example, always requires two coats of shellac.

Gesso

Acrylic gesso in liquid form is a chalky white paint that provides a smooth surface for gilding. It is most often used on surfaces like wood and bisque-fired ceramics. Gesso can be coloured by mixing with acrylic paints, pigments or toners.

Gesso can be applied with a range of tools, good quality brushes or foam applicators. Foam applicators, often used in the application of sealers for découpage, are a handy tool for applying gesso on some surfaces because they do not leave brush marks.

Apply gesso with a one-way brushing action: place brush on, brush down then lift off. Leave to cure or harden. When thoroughly dry and cured, lightly sand until smooth, then apply the next coat.

Paint

A painted base coat serves two functions. It seals the surface and provides a base colour under the leaf. The colours you choose are critical to the piece because they will show through gaps and cracks in the leaf.

TIP

When applying shellac to paper or any other very porous surface, cover the surface first with vertical strokes. After twenty minutes apply another coat using horizontal strokes. This process, called 'cross-hatching', is necessary because paper is so absorbent and must be sealed well.

TROUBLE SHOOTING

If you have applied gilding milk and leaf to a piece, and then discover (when you realise that the leaf is not sticking) that the surface is more porous than you previously thought, there is a way out. Shellac areas where the leaf did not adhere. When thoroughly dry, apply more gilding milk and leaf to these areas.

There is a variety of acrylic, water-based paints on the market in a huge range of both artists' and house-paint colours. Stencilling paint and paint sticks are acceptable if stencilling a design on a piece.

'White out'.
Gesso over bisque-
fired ceramics and
tired china.

Apply paint with an applicator that will minimise brush strokes, such as ox-hair or sable brushes, foam applicators and natural sponges. Brush in a sweeping up and down movement, lifting the brush off after each stroke. This minimises brush strokes. Apply one or two coats. If sponging, use a drifting motion across the piece.

Sealer

Acrylic sealer or varnish can be used as a base coat. It can also be added to paint to strengthen it. This is particularly useful when working with very porous surfaces. Sealers are usually applied with brushes or foam applicators.

STEP 3: *APPLYING GILDING MILK*

Gilding milk is a white, non-toxic, water-based adhesive. Quicksize, another adhesive used for gilding, is basically the same as gilding milk. It can be applied in the same manner but may take a different time to become dry and not stay workable for as long as gilding milk. If using quicksize, follow directions on the bottle. The instructions in this book are specifically for the use of gilding milk.

Before applying the gilding milk, think carefully about the piece and how you want it to look, as gilding milk is applied only to the areas you want gilded. Before doing anything else, plan your design. For example, if your design requires a straight edge, mark out the required edge with masking tape; if you are using a stencilled design, attach the stencil before applying the gilding milk.

Application

1. Cover your work table with a heavy plastic sheet and put on latex gloves.
2. Wipe over the entire piece with a tack cloth to remove grit and dust particles.
3. Cut a small piece of sponge (about a 2 cm cube). I find the most economical way is to buy a car sponge then cut pieces off that.
4. Tip a small amount of gilding milk into a wide-bottomed container (one with a lid so that the milk keeps).
5. Dip a corner of the sponge into the milk. Don't saturate the sponge. Wipe the milk onto the piece with a light up and down motion, rather than a rubbing, circular motion. Wipe over the piece (or areas) systematically, going over the surface twice to ensure a good coverage. It may be necessary to re-dip the sponge, but don't allow puddles to form or bubbles to stay on the surface.
6. After approximately 15 minutes, the surface of the piece will be tacky and workable, ready for the leaf. Test this by touching the surface with your finger. Remove gloves. If the surface feels wet and some milk comes off on your finger, it isn't ready. If it feels tacky and your finger remains dry, the surface is ready to gild. Wash your hands after testing, as the milk will become sticky on your fingers. Gilding milk dries clear. On some surfaces this is another indication that the surface is ready and workable. Under cool conditions, milk will be tacky and the surface will stay workable for up to two weeks. In hot, humid conditions the

milk behaves differently, so in these circumstances you will need to experiment and use your own judgement to assess if it is workable.

6. Discard the latex gloves and clean the plastic sheet with methylated spirits for re-use. The sponge may be re-used.

Gesso and leaf.

Terracotta fish, painted and gilded with variegated leaf.

STEP 4: *BUYING, CHOOSING AND APPLYING THE LEAF*

Buying gold, silver and metal leaf

Leaf can be purchased in transfer books or books of loose leaves. In transfer books, each sheet of leaf is mounted onto backing paper of either waxed or tissue paper. In books of loose leaves, each sheet of leaf is interleaved with tissue paper, but not mounted on backing paper. I prefer to buy genuine gold and metal leaf in transfer books as it is easier to use this way. The gilding method described in this book assumes that each sheet of leaf is mounted on backing paper. As you become more familiar with the texture and qualities of genuine gold and metal leaf you may find that eventually you prefer to buy it in books of loose leaves.

Gold leaf

Genuine 12-24-carat gold leaf comes in sheets 80 x 80 mm, in books of 25 leaves. The gold and silver leaf used in this book is genuine Australian gold and silver leaf, beaten locally to a micron thickness. The colour range is:

- white gold, 12 carat
- lemon gold, 16 carat
- green gold, 18 carat
- gold, 22 and 24 carat
- red gold, 23½ carat

Silver leaf

Silver leaf is available in sheets 95 x 95 mm, in books of 25 leaves. The silver leaf used in this book is genuine silver.

Metal leaf

Metal leaf comes in sheets 140 x 140 mm, in books of 25 leaves.
Metal leaf range is:

- imitation gold or Dutch metal
- copper
- aluminium
- variegated metal leaf

The variegated leaf comes in red, green, blue, black, autumnal tints and Atlantic tints and has a stippled or marbled look. The look of pewter can be obtained by using aluminium or silver leaf covered lightly with shoe polish and rottenstone. Metal leaf is thicker, stronger and cheaper than genuine gold leaf. The cost of leaf varies depending on the thickness, its country of origin and the supplier.

Choosing the right leaf for your piece

Your choice of colour and type of leaf depends on the size of the piece (which will affect the cost), the surface (whether it is relatively smooth or has recesses and mouldings, which will create more fractures), and the desired effect (colour, brightness, an aged, fractured look versus an evenly gilded look). You might want to use a gilded piece in your home decor to complete an effect you are creating. For example, if you have copper pots in the kitchen you may want to copperise a glass bottle to blend in with the character of the room. If you are gilding an art piece, choose a leaf that ties in well with the story you are telling. Also take into consideration the context of any gilding work. Folk art techniques such as découpage and paper tole can be enhanced using leaf. The possibilities are endless.

Should you select gold leaf or metal leaf? 12-24 carat gold leaf behaves in a different way from metal leaf. Gold leaf adheres more strongly to the backing

paper but, once laid on the piece, it fractures more easily. To achieve a more solid gold profile you can lay two or three sheets down directly on top of each other. Because of its fragility, genuine gold leaf produces subtle differences in colour definition and leaf density, depending on the surface used. Dutch metal, however, always looks the same regardless of the surface because it is a stronger, denser medium. It is also very bright, so if you want to produce the appearance of genuine gold, use a light gold-coloured gilding cream over the Dutch metal, working this gently over the leaf as described in the section on gilding creams. This dulls the brightness. The same applies to variegated, copper, silver and aluminium leaf.

Storing leaf

Between work sessions, store the leaf under a heavy object. This helps keep the leaf attached to the backing paper. I use a 15 cm square ceramic tile, which is gilded with a leaf from the book that it's sitting on. That way I know which book is which and can easily remind myself of the different colours.

Hints for beginners

Before tackling your first piece, keep the following points in mind.

1. Start with small projects like a food-colouring bottle, an egg or a small box (papier mâché or plastic). These three pieces provide an introduction to different surfaces and different-shaped pieces.
2. Start with metal leaf mounted on backing paper. It is stronger and handles better, providing an easier introduction to the process and the medium. For beginners, it is best to start with Dutch metal, variegated or aluminium leaf. Once you have developed some skill and understanding of metal leaf, move on to genuine gold and silver.
3. Always use leaf gently. Be aware of its fragility and its potential to crease and fold on itself. If this happens, blow softly straight down on the creased areas. You should be able to return the sheet to its square format without breaking it. Be careful not to work in a draught.
4. Fingerprints can initiate tarnishing. Don't be tempted to handle leaf without wearing cotton gloves.
5. Work the leaf close to the piece you are applying it to.

Applying the leaf

1. Lay a sheet of heavy white paper over your work surface.
2. Put on cotton gloves.
3. Once you've decided which leaf to use, take a sheet out of the book by inserting your hand under the backing paper and pulling it out gently so the leaf doesn't fly off.
4. Decide exactly where you want the leaf to go. Lay the leaf face down onto the desired area. It will stick immediately on contact with the gilding milk. Do not try to move it sideways.

Raw wood mirror, copperised on a raw wood gold easel; polished wood copperised candle holder.

5. Smooth your gloved finger over the backing paper to make sure the leaf has adhered to the surface.

6. Lift or slide off the backing paper.

7. Take a clean, soft brush and tamp the leaf firmly onto the surface. A cosmetic blusher brush works well.

8. If you only need a portion of a sheet of leaf, sandwich it between two layers of backing paper. Lay this sandwich on the work bench. Don't hold it in your hand. Now, cut it with very sharp scissors or a very fine scalpel, taking care not to drag through the paper. When using a scalpel, a cutting mat should be used. Remember, when cutting leaf to size, allow for approximately 5-10 mm of overlap. There's no going back with leaf, so it's better to be generous with your measurements to avoid unwanted gaps.

9. When the entire piece has been leafed, rub over the gilded area with your gloved finger or paint brush to remove any excess or skewings. Tip the skewings into a skewings box. Skewings are useful for filling gaps later on. Keep colours separate or mix them together in one box.

Joins

When applying a number of sheets side by side, particularly on a flat piece, joins are almost always visible. If your aim is to minimise the impact of the join, think carefully about where you place the first sheet. On a square item like a 15 cm square ceramic tile, you would place the first sheet of leaf in the bottom corner then patch around the remaining two sides. On a round surface, start anywhere along the edge and place the sheets on the diagonal. This creates a camouflage effect, which itself is an attractive pattern.

Creating a band of gold

If a band of gold is required, I've discovered an exceptionally easy, foolproof method using double-sided adhesive tape.

First, measure the length of band to be gilded and cut this amount off the role of tape. Do not remove the backing paper. To ensure a clean edge, place a layer of used waxed or tissue paper over the sheet of leaf you are about to use (in the same way as you would when cutting the leaf) leaving only the width of the band exposed. With sticky side facing down, place one end of the adhesive tape on the edge of the sheet of leaf with an ungloved hand (be careful not to stick the tape to the tissue paper that the leaf is mounted on). With the other gloved hand holding just enough tape to span the width of leaf, press the tape onto the leaf. Now, run your gloved finger along the tape to adhere the leaf to the tape evenly. Gently lift the band of leaf from the backing paper. Place the next section of tape to be gilded on the sheet of leaf, making sure there is approximately a 2 mm overlap. Work systematically up the sheet of leaf and along the tape, section by section, until the entire strip of tape is gilded.

Once the band of tape is gilded, rub gilding cream on if desired. If cracks occur because the leaf fractures, it is important to rub a finishing cream, such as gilding cream, beeswax polish or shoe polish over these areas to eliminate exposed sticky areas. These creams will change the colour of the leaf slightly.

Finally, seal the gilded tape with shellac or a sealer. When shellac is thoroughly dry, carefully peel off the backing tape to expose the adhesive, at the same time laying the gilded band on the piece, bit by bit. This prevents the tape folding and sticking to itself. To ensure precise placement, where possible, rule a faint line on the piece of work.

This method of leaf application is particularly useful for gilding paper. It eliminates the need for base coats and gilding milk which can cause paper to become stressed. Double-sided tape has magic qualities that can be widely used for craft projects.

As well as straight bands of leaf, double-sided tape can be used to cut out small shapes. First, gild a band or strip, then cut out your shape. For example, if cutting out a symmetrical image such as a heart, slip a piece of scrap paper inside the fold to ensure the raw edges don't stick together when cut. Cut out the heart, open out the shape and remove the piece of paper. Peel off the backing paper and stick down the shape.

Stencilling

Leaf can be applied through a stencil to achieve regular, repeated designs. Stencils can be bought pre-cut or you can cut your own using stencil paper, acetate or mylar. Stencils can be used in reverse or upside down.

Using a pre-cut stencil, lightly apply a repositionable spray adhesive to the back of the stencil then attach it to the area you wish to gild. Hold the stencil down firmly with masking tape. Apply gilding milk to the cut-out area of the stencil. When tacky, apply leaf and any finishing creams. Lift off the stencil, clean it, then repeat this process until the desired effect is achieved. Finally, seal the entire piece with an appropriate sealer.

Note: The stencil patterns used in this book are given on page 76.

TROUBLE SHOOTING

If you don't like the leaf that you have just applied, you can apply more gilding milk over the leaf then apply a different leaf on top of the original one.

Bands of gold highlight several pieces to give a 'less is more' approach.

STEP 5: *FINISHES AND DECORATIVE EFFECTS*

My experience over the last ten years of gilding and running gilding workshops has helped me devise and experiment with different finishes. Softening or changing a look to cover mistakes is an art form in itself. Few people make the right choices and apply the leaf to the right areas the first time around. Everybody makes mistakes, and with gold and metal leaf (except on a few surfaces like china, plastic and glass) once the leaf is applied there is no turning back. Once it's on, it's on! For this reason, using and experimenting with a variety of finishes is an essential part of gilding.

Finishes

Finishes that you can apply to gold or metal leaf include:

- finishing creams (gilding cream, shoe polish, beeswax polish and artists' oils)
- asphaltum
- rottenstone
- modelling or texture paste
- crackle medium

Finishing creams

Finishing creams are creams that are rubbed over the leaf to subdue the brightness or change the colour of the leaf. Rubbing on a finishing cream also changes the colour of any base coat showing through fractures in the leaf. A final coat or sealer is applied over the finishing cream.

- Gilding cream is used by furniture makers, framers (to restore gilded pieces) and other craftspeople to buff up wooden surfaces. I use it as a finish after gilding to give an evenly gilded look, or to achieve tonal gold on gold qualities between the gilded and ungilded areas. Each brand (I list brands on page 18) has a range of gold and other colours.

- Artists' oils and shoe polish are used in instances where you wish to highlight the base colour that shows through the leaf or create a new colour to accessorise the leaf. It is possible to mix the particular colour you want using artists' oil paints. This is then rubbed sparingly on the gilded or ungilded areas with a rag. Similarly, shoe polish (one with a sponge applicator like Padawax is best) can be used to subdue the brightness of metal leaf (see photograph on page 32 of the copper mirror, where shoe polish was rubbed sparingly over copper leaf). Black shoe polish rubbed over aluminium leaf gives the look of pewter.

- Beeswax polish is a clear polish that produces little colour variation in the leaf. It can be buffed up to a glow.

Apply finishing creams using a rag, lightly dipping it in the cream, shoe polish or paint. Wipe or stroke the rag gently over the area, following the directions of the surface curves or moulds. Buff up to a glow. Don't try to buff up artists' oils as they will not give a sheen.

Asphaltum

Asphaltum (bituminous black) is thinned, liquid asphalt, which can give a tortoiseshell finish to the piece. It can be bought in tins from paint shops as bituminous black paint. Dilute it by mixing one part bituminous black to nine parts of turpentine. Bituminous black or asphaltum can be stippled, sponged or sprayed over gilded areas. Each method gives a slightly different tortoiseshell-like effect. Asphaltum can be applied directly onto the leaf or over a coat of shellac; the latter gives a more speckledy look.

NOTE: You must work outside with this substance and wear latex gloves.

● **Stippling**

Stippling gives a fur-like appearance. Use a dry, preferably round brush with firm bristles. Dip it into asphaltum mixture, then dab off any excess on a folded paper towel, leaving a semi-loaded, dry brush. Lightly dab the brush up and down in drifts on the desired areas. This action is called 'stippling'. Always stipple in irregular drifts rather than in regular patterns.

● **Sponging**

Sponging gives a lacy appearance. Using a small, natural sea sponge, dampen the sponge with a tiny quantity of water so that it becomes pliable. Choose an area of sponge that has an open, lacy texture. Gently dunk this area into the asphaltum mixture, then dab off the excess on a folded paper towel. This process serves two functions: it removes the excess and shows you the lacy patterning and density of colour that will be achieved. If you are happy with the effect, dab the semi-loaded sponge on the desired areas.

● **Spraying**

Spraying or misting the asphaltum on gives a speckledy effect. First, buy a plastic spray bottle with an adjustable nozzle. Test the density of the spray with some turpentine. Spray it on to a sheet of coloured paper, which will show up the misting qualities of the sprayer. Adjust the nozzle to the spray density required.

Pour the bituminous black and turpentine mixture into the spray bottle. Work outdoors, wearing gloves and preferably a mask, too. Also, work over a clean plastic sheet so that the excess doesn't drip all over the ground. Hold or place the piece approximately a metre away. The closer you are, the less definition is achieved. If the piece is three-dimensional, devise a way of supporting it so that it can be sprayed from every angle. Test the asphaltum spray on paper to check that the texture and density of colour is right before you begin.

● **Combining techniques**

You can combine stippling, sponging and spraying in any combination without waiting for the asphaltum to dry. Remember to apply it conservatively, building up the effect gradually. If, however, you do need to remove some areas, do so with a sponge.

Wait until the asphaltum is totally dry (this may take some time, maybe two to four weeks, depending on the weather), before applying the final coat.

Rottenstone

Rottenstone is powdered limestone and it can be bought from gilding suppliers. It produces a soft, grey-green effect so the piece appears aged and dusty. It is used to highlight recesses where dust would naturally gather and is best applied over the final shellac coat while it is still tacky. Dust the rottenstone on with a bone-dry brush.

NOTE: Blow off any dust and clean around the area with a cotton bud.

Create an 18th century look using papers and asphaltum.

Modelling or texture paste

Modelling paste is particularly useful on vertical decorative surfaces. It can be applied over the base coat or the raw surface, creating a rough textured surface. It dries hard so that when leaf is applied over the top, it cracks and fractures.

Apply the paste straight from the jar with a dry brush or the tip of a small palette knife. Either dab it on for a rough texture or smooth it on for a less textured look. Paste can be diluted with a little water but keep in mind that it should be firm enough to retain its shape when applied. Don't over apply or it will tend to crack as it dries.

Paint over the dried paste if desired. If not, apply gilding milk and leaf directly onto the paste. Cracks will appear as the leaf fractures.

Crackle medium

There are a number of different substances on the market that will give a cracked, antiqued effect to painted surfaces. Each crackle medium works slightly differently. In some cases it is applied underneath the paint layer, in other cases it is applied onto the gilded surface. In each case the crackle medium forces cracks to appear in the surface. Depending on how much crackle medium is applied, the cracks are hair-line or quite wide.

Apply crackle medium following directions for the particular brand used.

Decorative effects

Decorations that can be used to enhance gilded pieces include:

- three-dimensional effects
- illustrative effects
- painted images

Three-dimensional effects

Mouldings, buttons, beads, ornaments, junk jewellery (taken apart and the bits used), seeds, seed pods, small sea-washed pebbles, fragments of broken mirror or tiles, driftwood, shells, nuts in their shells, knobs, car parts (washers, nuts and bolts), computer parts (microchips)...

There is such a huge range of bits and bobs that can be used to decorate gilded pieces, the list could go on forever. Glue these decorations on either before the piece is base coated, if you want to gild over the decoration, or after the piece is gilded if you do not want the decoration covered in leaf. Choose a glue appropriate to the surface and the decoration. You can glue decorative effects directly on to the leaf or the final coat.

Illustrative effects

Two-dimensional effects, such as decals, transfers or the paper cut-outs that are used for découpage, can be applied directly onto the leaf before the final coat. Apply the final coat over entire piece, including the decorative effect. Dry-transfer lettering, such as Letraset or Decadry can be applied either before or after the final coat.

A silver seaside story with surface decoration.

I wandered lonely as a cloud
that floats on high o'er vales and hills,
when all at once I saw a crowd,
A host of Golden daffodils,
William Wordsworth 1770-1850

A memoir painted by Jane Devine matched with appropriate fabric and touches of 22ct gold leaf.

Painted images

Various paints can be used on different surfaces to add design over the leaf. On glass and ceramic (including ceramic tiles) use Deco Art Ultra Gloss acrylic enamel paint (Pioneer Craft). This paint, when baked in the oven gives a durable, gloss enamel look that is dishwasher safe. It can be used to paint designs over the leaf. Be sure to follow the directions on the paint for the temperatures for baking.

On other surfaces use artists' oils and acrylic paints. First apply a sealer of the same brand as the paint. Then, once the painted design is dry, seal again.

STEP 6: *THE FINAL COAT*

Applying a final sealing coat over the gilded piece is an essential step in the gilding process, because it stops the leaf wearing off and tarnishing. The sealer can be shellac or an acrylic sealer.

Shellac

Shellac is probably the most common sealer. Different colours give different effects. Blonde shellac or the pre-mixed blonde de-waxed shellac gives a warm glow to the gold with minimal change of colour. Shellac is applied as described in Step 2. Wear latex gloves and apply with a bob to minimise brush strokes.

Fishy tiles with copper leaf. Gilded avocado pips with pomegranates complement the gilded china plate and nutcracker.

Sealer

A clear acrylic sealer is also used as a final coat on some surfaces. The sealer can be coloured with a variety of substances — acrylic paint, metallic powders, pigments, stains, even with skewings of leaf. Application is the same as for paints. Use the best quality brush or foam applicator to minimise brush strokes. Spray

*In the kitchen.
Find the gilded
accessories.*

mist sealers in aerosol spray cans are useful to eliminate brush strokes.

Where possible, dip small or circular pieces into the sealer or shellac holding them with tweezers, instead of using a bob or a brush. Let the excess drip off, then leave them standing independently to dry. This eliminates brush strokes altogether.

The Workshops

Gilding a picture frame is a project that should be treated with the utmost respect, as it not only frames the work but must stand on its own merit. Choose your frame carefully for its style and purpose. It may have embossed raised surfaces or cracks in the wood. Gilding can transform it completely and enhance the frame's suitability for the art work within it. Choose carefully the base colour, which will show through cracks in the leaf. The base colour, the leaf and any finishing creams applied over the leaf should all work well together — each highlighting or complementing the other. This is important.

MATERIALS AND TOOLS REQUIRED FOR THIS WORKSHOP

Optional finishes and decorative effects are not included in this list. See *Materials and Tools* and *The Basics* for details of these.

Bob
Gesso
Gilding milk
Cotton gloves
Latex gloves
Leaf
Paint *(coloured acrylic and artists' oil paints)*
Paint brushes
Paper *(heavy weight to cover work surface)*
Plastic sheet *(to cover work surface)*
Sandpaper
Shellac
Sponge
Tack cloth
Wood filler
(if necessary)

Before it can begin.

WORKSHOP 1

wood

Traditionally, picture frames are gilded using the water-gilding method involving four base coats of bole, each one carefully sanded back to provide as smooth a surface as possible. The frame is then gilded only with 22-carat gold and finally burnished to a glow with the agate stone. This produces a perfectly smooth, unfractured look that has a depth of colour and glow unachievable with my method. The 22-carat gold leaf applied on top of the base coats described in this book cannot be burnished with an agate stone. Without the

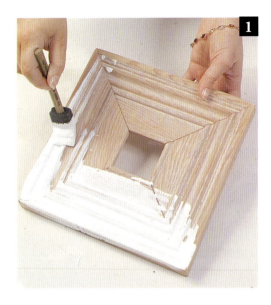

layers of bole, the agate simply scratches and wears away the leaf. However, gold leaf applied to a picture frame base coated with gesso instead of bole will give you an aged gold effect or a soft glowing effect which still looks wonderful, requires much less work and is environmentally friendly. But don't expect it to look the same as a frame gilded by an artisan using traditional gilding methods.

RAW WOOD

Gilding a new picture frame

Preparation
Cover the work surface with a plastic cloth. Fill any holes with wood filler. Clean and sand the frame until smooth.

1. Base coat
Seal the whole surface with two coats of gesso leaving ample drying and hardening time between coats. When thoroughly dry, lightly sand until smooth to touch.

2. Using acrylic paint, choose a base colour or colours. The frame shown on this page was base painted with black and a good, bright red. The black was brushed on selected irregular areas. When this was dry, the remaining areas were painted red. It was then lightly sanded.

Wearing latex gloves, shellac the painted frame with a bob (as described in *The Basics*). Leave until quite dry.

Note: For an American country look, use a storm-blue base coat painted irregularly with black. Pine-green base coat with black gives a weathered garden look. Yellow ochre and storm-blue gives a French country look.

3. Applying gilding milk
Apply gilding milk as described in *The Basics*.

4. Applying the leaf
Wearing cotton gloves and working over a clean sheet of paper, remove one page of leaf from the book with its backing paper attached. Alternatively, cut the binding from the book if using all the leaves. (See *The Basics* for a more detailed description of working with the leaf.)

Lay one edge of the leaf on the outer edge of a corner of the frame. Using a tamping motion, gently run your fingers or a cosmetic blusher brush over the backing paper so that the leaf sticks to the frame. Lift off the backing paper. Apply to the next sheet of leaf, overlapping each section by as much as 5 mm.

If the frame is narrow, cut the leaf into the appropriate size strips as described in *The Basics*. If the frame is moulded, allow a little extra for the leaf to settle into the grooves. When the entire area is gilded, tamp with a paint brush or gloved finger to ensure the leaf has adhered well and to remove skewings.

If the frame is moulded, lay the sheet starting at the outer edge, gently tamping the leaf into recessed areas with a paint brush or gloved finger. Step leaf down the frame working from the outer edge to the inner edge. Remove backing paper and, using a brush or finger, tamp the leaf into the grooves.

Cracks will appear in the leaf. These are unavoidable, especially when working with genuine gold. These can be touched up with skewings or gilding cream if you want the look to be even. Don't forget that base paint colours showing through the cracks looks effective.

5. Finishes and decorative effects
Use of finishes and decorative effects depends entirely on the look you are after. If the frame is gilded with genuine gold and you want a rich, reflective finish, leave the piece as it is, applying only a final sealing coat.

However, if you want a tonal, gold on gold aged look, apply a classical gold-coloured gilding cream sparingly to the entire piece. This gives a gold look to the base coat colour showing through leaf fractures and reduces the reflective quality of the leaf. Buff with a clean cloth.

If the frame has been gilded with Dutch metal, which is brighter than genuine gold, the effect may need to be dulled. Black shoe polish (Padawax) can be applied sparingly. This mops up the brightness and gives a dark, stained look to any base coat showing through. If gilding cream is applied first, the shoe polish sticks more easily, giving a more pronounced aged effect.

6. Final coat
Apply a light coat of shellac with a bob. Alternatively, mist or spray on a sealer. Spraying avoids brush strokes.

Gilded eggs.

RAW WOOD

Wooden eggs

The egg has broad decorative appeal. Gilded wooden or marble eggs gleam when displayed in ornamental bowls or plates. This workshop gives you the opportunity to play with an object that is timeless and elegant, but not precious or unique. With these eggs you can try out different effects, different finishes, different types and combinations of leaf. Experiment with plaster, papier mâché, plastic and blown eggs as well as wooden eggs.

Base coat

If the surface is raw wood, apply two coats of acrylic paint or gesso. Allow these to dry thoroughly between coats.

Applying gilding milk

Apply as described in *The Basics*.

Applying the leaf

Experiment with different types and colours of leaf. Place the leaf (with the backing paper still attached) in the palm of your gloved hand. Put the egg on the leaf then wrap the leaf around it.

Another gilding method that achieves quite a different effect is to drop the egg into your skewings box or jar. Jiggle the egg inside the container until entirely covered with skewings. Take it out and then rub off the excess with a gloved hand.

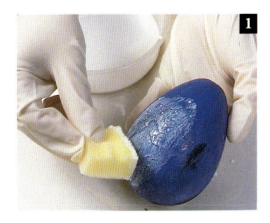

Finishes and decorative effects

Here are a number of optional finishes and decorative effects you can play around with.

• Decals can be applied directly on the leaf. Soak the decal in water until it comes off the transfer paper. Smooth it on the flattest area of the egg to ensure no wrinkles, or cut small slits into the edge of decal and overlap these areas to fit the curves of the egg. Leave at least two or three hours for the gum to dry.

• Découpage by gluing paper cut-outs directly on the leaf.

• Apply gilding cream to achieve an even coverage of gold or to give an aged-gold tonal look, with the cracked areas contrasting with the gilded areas. You can apply an ultra-thin layer of gilding cream over a decal or découpaged area.

• Paint images by applying any artists' oil or acrylic paints over the leaf once the leaf has been sealed. First, apply a sealer over the leaf. Use a sealer of the same brand as the paint you are using. Paint on your design. Once it is thoroughly dry, apply a final coat of sealer.

• Asphaltum, or bituminous black, gives a tortoiseshell look. Mist, sponge or stipple on as described in *The Basics*.

Final coat

Seal the egg with shellac, or a spray with a sealer, to minimise brush strokes. Use a suitable sealer for the work, bearing in mind the particular decorative effects used.

MDF AND RAW CORK

Treat in the same way as raw wood.

PAINTED WOOD

Preparation

If the painted surface shows signs of wear, sand these areas back to the raw wood. Fill any holes with a wood sealer if you want a perfectly even surface. If no preparation is required, apply gilding milk directly on the painted surface.

Base coat

If after preparation raw areas are exposed, seal these with a sealer that is consistent with the original paint work.

Applying gilding milk

Apply as described in *The Basics*.

Applying the leaf

Apply as described in *The Basics*. If gilding a painted picture frame, refer to page 48 for details on gilding frames.

Finishes and decorative effects

Apply as desired, referring to *The Basics* for details.

Final coat

Apply a sealer that is appropriate to the piece.

POLISHED AND WAXED WOOD

Preparation

Sand back areas that show signs of wear.

Base coat

In the case of polished wood, apply a stain that matches the original colour to any raw areas exposed after preparation. In the case of waxed wood, re-wax or re-polish exposed areas.

Applying gilding milk and the leaf

Apply as described in *The Basics*.

Finishes and decorative effects

Apply as desired, referring to *The Basics* for details.

Final coat

Apply a sealer that is appropriate to the piece.

LAMINATED CORK

Laminated cork items that you might consider gilding include place mats and coasters.

Base coat

As the cork is already sealed, no base coat is required. However, if the surface is scratched and worn, apply one coat of shellac or a sealer.

Applying gilding milk and the leaf

Apply as described in *The Basics*.

Finishes and decorative effects

Apply as desired, referring to *The Basics* for details.

Final coat

Use an appropriate sealer and as many coats as necessary to protect against heat.

Gilding for Christmas.

Old bottles, new bottles, clear bottles, blue bottles.

WORKSHOP 2

glass

MATERIALS AND TOOLS REQUIRED FOR THIS WORKSHOP

Optional finishes and decorative effects are not included in this list. See *Materials and Tools* and *The Basics* for details of these.

Bob
Gilding milk
Latex gloves
Cotton gloves
Leaf
Methylated spirits *(cleaning only)*
Paint brushes
Paper *(heavy weight to cover work surface)*
Plastic sheet *(to cover work surface)*
Shellac
Sponge
Tack cloth.

Bottles – old bottles, new bottles, tiny medicine bottles, liqueur bottles, bottles of all shapes and sizes – are the obvious glass pieces to gild. Their distinctive shape is enhanced a hundredfold when gilded. Food essence bottles (25-50 ml) and small glass medicine bottles look wonderful gilded with a decorative glass stopper, such as a piece of cork with a decorative piece glued to the top.

Preparation
Clean the surface thoroughly. If necessary use methylated spirits and a rag.

Base coat
As glass is a sealed, non-porous surface there is no need to apply a base coat.

Applying gilding milk
Using a small piece of sponge, wipe the milk on the bottle in a systematic way (for example, from top to bottom, always wiping in the same direction). Remember to apply milk to the bottom of the bottle, standing the bottle on its neck to do this. See *The Basics* for more details.

If milk has been applied to an unwanted area, or if you change your mind about the areas you want gilded,

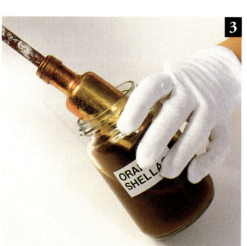

wipe off the gilding milk with methylated spirits and a rag.

Applying the leaf

For a 375 ml drink bottle you will need approximately two sheets of Dutch metal, more if using 22-carat gold leaf. Place one sheet of leaf with the backing paper still attached to the work surface (leaf facing up). Place the bottom edge of the bottle in line with the bottom edge of the leaf and, starting at one side, roll the bottle along the leaf. The leaf will adhere to the glass immediately. Pick up the bottle and gently smooth the leaf down with a gloved finger. If the leaf did not entirely wrap around the bottle, cut the next sheet of leaf to the desired width, allowing for an overlap of up to 5 mm. Apply this strip in the same manner. See *The Basics* for more details on cutting and applying leaf.

If small cracks appear in the leaf, these can be touched up by applying a small amount of gilding milk to the patches of glass, then applying more leaf. Use skewings for these small areas.

Final coat

Wearing latex gloves, apply two coats of shellac. This can be done with a bob. To avoid finger prints, support the bottle by placing a skewer inside the opening. Alternatively, dip the gilded bottle in shellac, supporting it with a brush handle jammed tightly into the neck of the bottle. Choose the appropriate colour shellac for the desired effect. Leave approximately twenty minutes drying time between coats.

WORKSHOP 3

metal

Applying metal or gold leaf to an existing metal surface is an unusual application of gilding techniques. Unlike plastic, where the aim is usually to cover the surface entirely, such camouflaging is not necessary with metal. The texture and lustre of a metal surface has attractive qualities and patterns – and leaf can further enhance these. Adding a touch of leaf, such as a band of gold around a watering can, adds warmth, lustre and a touch of elegance to an already lustrous surface. Tin, with its lightness, strength and both decorative and functional uses, is definitely worthy of consideration when choosing a piece to gild.

There is a wide range of metal surfaces you could consider gilding: raw or polished tinware, wrought iron, raw or painted metal, aluminium, anodised aluminium, stainless steel. Watering cans, cookie cutters, stainless steel cutlery, anodised aluminium cups and coasters, tin trays and bowls are all possibilities. The list could extend to brass, copper, silver and pewter, particularly pieces that have become discoloured and lost their original appeal. Bear in mind with treasures like these, that 'less is more' and a touch of leaf goes a long way.

RAW TINWARE
Preparation
Clean with turpentine and a rag. If any rust is apparent, use a rust converter (such as Killrust) to stop it from spreading.

Base coat
The metal piece you have chosen to gild may have been finished or sealed in any number of ways that you won't know about. The best approach to ensure

successful gilding is to seal all metal pieces, except stainless steel and anodised aluminium, with a clear sealer. Seal the entire piece, even if leaf is only going to be applied to some areas.

Applying gilding milk and the leaf
Apply as described in *The Basics*. Remember, decorating tinware with simple bands of gold or a stencilled pattern can achieve a deceptively delicate look.

Final coat
Apply a coat of acrylic all-weather sealer to the entire piece.

STAINLESS STEEL
Gilding old stainless steel cutlery (do gild the handles only) from opportunity shops gives a whole new lease of life to these otherwise tired-looking household items. Any patterns on the stainless steel handles show clearly through the leaf. Remember never to put these treasures in the dishwasher once they are gilded.

Preparation
Clean with methylated spirits and, if necessary, use steel wool to remove any stains or grit.

Base coat
Not required.

Applying gilding milk and the leaf
Apply as described in *The Basics*. Remember to apply gilding milk and leaf only to the handles. Use masking tape for a clear definition between gilded and ungilded areas. Put the tape on before applying the milk and remove after the final coat has dried.

Finishes and decorative effects
You can utilise oddments from old cutlery sets (including cutlery with plastic and wooden handles), turning them into ornamental pieces (such as ornamental spoons) or specialised pieces (such as cake knives). Do this by gluing decorations to the handle either at the beginning of the gilding process (if they are to be gilded over) or at the end of the process, if the decoration is not to be gilded. (See *The Basics* for more details.)

Final coat
Apply a clear sealer or shellac chosen to complement the colour of the leaf. Holding the ungilded end of the knife, fork or spoon, dip the handle into the sealer. Once the excess has dripped off, stand the piece upside down in a jar to dry.

ANODISED ALUMINIUM
Treat in exactly the same way as stainless steel.

Tinware, anodised aluminium stencilled or banded with gold.

WORKSHOP 4

plastics

This workshop applies to all kinds of acrylic, perspex and plastic. Such things as plastic plates, cups, jewellery, curtain rings, ornaments, plastic doilies and table cloths, window dressing forms, cosmetic jars, plastic containers and serviette rings are all amenable to gilding. The possibilities are endless. Because plastic is so commonplace, scratches easily and is not necessarily intended to last, I am always keen to try and transform it into something else, giving it a new lease of life instead of throwing it out.

Plastic, unlike any other surface, is often coloured, so with very little effort interesting effects can be produced as the surface colour shows through the leaf. When choosing a plastic piece to gild, make sure the original shape and surface design is attractive, because gilding cannot change that. Look also for any raised or recessed areas that will be an interesting feature.

Preparation
Clean thoroughly.

Base coat
Not required.

Applying gilding milk
Apply gilding milk as described in *The Basics*.

Applying the leaf
On a round surface such as a plastic plate, apply the leaf in an angular manner so the leaf becomes a pattern in itself. Start by adhering one corner of a sheet to

TROUBLE SHOOTING

With plastic surfaces, if you don't like the result, the milk and leaf can be removed by rubbing with methylated spirits and a cloth.

A contemporary approach to silver.

the lip of the plate, then allow the rest of the leaf to stick. Repeat these diamond shapes over the whole plate. Try combining different coloured leaves together; for example, white gold, lemon gold or silver with 22-carat gold, to accentuate the angles. If the plate is coloured and you wish the colour to show through, leave some ungilded areas.

Finishes and decorative effects

Apply as desired, referring to *The Basics* for details.

As plastic is such a smooth, non-porous surface, gilding cream cannot be applied to the original plastic surface. This means that gaps in the leaf cannot be touched up with cream. If an evenly gilded look is required, apply more gilding milk and leaf to any ungilded areas.

Final coat

Apply one coat of sealer or shellac to tone with the colour of the leaf.

WORKSHOP 5

ceramics

Deco art ultra gloss over china and glass.

This workshop covers china, bisque-fired ceramics, terracotta pots and planters. Other possibilities are porcelain ornaments and decorative china such as teapots, cups and saucers or mugs. If you have an attractively shaped piece but dislike its colour, the colour can be eliminated by applying up to three coats of *gesso*. Once the gesso is sealed, the piece can be gilded as desired.

CHINA

China plates and glazed ceramic tiles can be gilded for decorative purposes or for use as underplates to be used under soup or dinner plates. It is not advisable to use gilded plates to serve food on or where constant cleaning is required. For light cleaning, wipe over with a damp cloth. Never put gilded plates in the dishwasher.

Preparation
Clean thoroughly.

Base coat
None required.

Applying gilding milk and the leaf
Apply as described in *The Basics*.

As china is such a smooth, non-porous surface, gilding milk and leaf can be rubbed off with methylated spirits and a rag. This is good if you make mistakes or change your mind. On the other hand, it means you cannot rub gilding cream on the ceramic surface to touch up bare spots. For this reason, if you

want an even coverage of leaf with as few cracks as possible, it is better to use metal leaf and apply gilding cream to subdue the brightness rather than use the more fragile gold or silver leaf.

Alternatively, use genuine gold leaf and keep adding more gilding milk and leaf to cover up fractures and gaps.

Finishes
Gilding cream can be rubbed on gilded areas as a finishing cream, but be careful not to rub too hard. Asphaltum can be applied for a tortoiseshell look.

Decorative effects
Designs can be painted on plates and ceramic tiles using Deco Art Ultra Gloss (see *The Basics* for details).

Final coat
Apply a sealer or shellac appropriate to the piece.

BISQUE-FIRED CERAMIC
Base coat
Two base coats will ensure a well-sealed surface. Use paint, gesso, shellac or a combination of the three.

Applying gilding milk and the leaf
Apply as described in *The Basics*.

Finishes
Apply as desired, referring to *The Basics* for details.

Final coat
Use shellac or a sealer to suit the colour of the piece.

TERRACOTTA
Preparation
Clean the surface thoroughly.

Base coat
Terracotta is a porous surface, so it must be sealed first with at least one coat of acrylic paint or two coats of shellac or sealer.

Paint has more possibilities because you can apply different colours to different areas, giving interesting effects as the colour shows through cracks in the leaf.

Consider using distemper on terracotta pots, as the colours are so distinctive. However, if distemper is used as a base coat, a coat of shellac over the distemper is advisable to ensure a well-sealed surface. If distemper is left unsealed, the weather will change its colour; this in itself is interesting to observe over time.

Applying gilding milk and the leaf

Apply as described in *The Basics*. If gilding terracotta pots, a simple band of leaf or stencilled patterns around the rim of a plain banded pot looks effective.

Finishes and decorative effects

Apply as desired, referring to *The Basics* for details.

Final coat

Use an acrylic all-weather sealer to protect it outdoors.

A blue base-painted variegated leaf terracotta planter.

WORKSHOP 6

other surfaces

There is a myriad of surfaces out in the world to decorate. Here is a selection of different material surfaces for you to approach. They range from paper and papier mâché to plaster, concrete, stone – and even leather.

Check each different surface for materials and tools required.

PAPIER MÂCHÉ

As there is now an endless variety of objects in papier mâché, only a few pieces have been gilded as examples. A feature of these pieces is the variety of three-dimensional decorative pieces that have been added either before or after the gilding process. The many different shapes and sizes of boxes in papier mâché offer great potential for creative and personalised packaging.

Preparation

Glue on any decorations that are to be gilded using a glue appropriate to the surface and the decoration.

Base coat

As papier mâché is very porous, it must be well sealed. Seal with an acrylic sealer or acrylic paint. If using sealer, mix paint with the sealer to give a base colour which will show through the cracks. Apply two coats, leaving ample drying time between coats.

From chocolate boxes to hat boxes, and beyond.

Opposite, concrete bases and silver leaf. Terracotta pots made to look like tin, using aluminium leaf and shoe polish.

If desired, paint inside the box with the same base colour. Seal with a clear acrylic sealer.

Applying gilding milk and the leaf
Apply as described in *The Basics*.

Finishes
Apply as desired, referring to *The Basics* for details.

Decorative effects
See *The Basics* for ideas. Glue ungilded decorations on, either before or after the final coat, as desired.

Final Coat
Apply a clear sealer or shellac to suit the colour of the piece.

PLASTER
Preparation
Sand rough edges with a fine-grained sandpaper. Do this outside, wearing face protection.

Base coat
Apply two coats of acrylic paint.

Applying gilding milk and the leaf
Apply as described in *The Basics*.

Finishes and decorative effects
Apply as desired, referring to *The Basics* for details.

Final coat
Seal with an acrylic all-weather sealer.

CONCRETE
Preparation
If the concrete is old, use a domestic bleach to kill any algae or moss that might be growing. Sand off any unwanted bits.

Base coat
Apply two coats of a sealer or paint according to the desired effect.

Applying gilding milk and the leaf
Apply as described in *The Basics*.

Finishes and decorative effects
Apply as desired, referring to *The Basics* for details.

Keepsakes.
Baby's first shoes.

Final coat
Seal for interior or exterior use with an all-weather sealer.

LEATHER

Base coat
If leather – shoes, bags, belts, gloves and chair seats – have already been tanned and coloured, the surface is sufficiently sealed for gilding.

Applying gilding milk and the leaf
Apply as described in *The Basics*.

Finishes
Apply gilding cream or a small quantity of shoe polish on a cotton rag, being careful to choose an appropriate colour. Don't use liquid shoe polish. For example, if using copper leaf, black shoe polish rubbed sparingly over the surface with a cotton rag accentuates the cracks and mops up the brightness.

Final coat
Ornamental leather pieces can be sealed with shellac for preservation. As wear-

able items may crack with a sealer, use gilding cream as a final coat and touch up areas that deteriorate with use.

SEA-WASHED STONE

Preparation
Oil the stone with household cooking oil. Outline the area to be gilded with masking tape.

Base coat
None required.

Stencilled sea-washed stone.

Applying gilding milk and the leaf

Apply gilding milk inside the masked area, then apply the leaf. Consider using 22-carat gold or genuine silver because they have a greater chance of surviving outdoors. Dutch metal and variegated leaf may tarnish and wear.

Final coat

Apply an all-weather sealer to the gilded area. Once this is done, remove the masking tape. The leaf should have a crisp edge with minimal fractures. Finally, to safeguard the leaf from chipping, apply another coat of sealer to the entire stone.

PAPER

When gilding paper, always put plastic under your work rather than paper.

Base coat

Paper is a very porous surface so it must be sealed with a strong clear acrylic sealer. Ultragrain is an excellent sealer for paper. Apply two coats in different directions for a stronger effect; that is, the first coat is applied using vertical strokes, the second coat is applied using horizontal strokes. Different papers will respond differently to sealers. Recycled paper will require sealing a number of times whereas paper doilies need only one coat. Matisse, Intergrain Ultraclear, Liquitex and Jo Sonja are clear sealers/varnishes that work well on paper, as does pre-mixed, white, de-waxed shellac. Apply with a foam applicator or brush.

Applying gilding milk and the leaf

The easiest way to add a touch of leaf to paper (for example, a band of gold or small shapes) is to use double-sided adhesive tape. This method is sometimes easier than stencilling. The technique, which doesn't require the application of base coats or gilding milk, is described in some detail in *The Basics*.

Beautiful paper for every purpose — from writing to packaging.

1829
Montgolfier, French paper
maker, introduced paper
table cloths and paper hangings
with embossed designs — known as
"papier-linge"

*Gilding the
men's room.*

THE FINAL WORD

opening Pandora's box

From seeds and stones to fabulous furniture, from plastic bangles to gilded staircases. Now you have the gilding bug and the technique, the possibilities are endless. This book has demonstrated the art of gilding by way of transforming small, economical, sometimes discarded household items into an array of treasured pieces of art. But there's no need to stop at small pieces. Be adventurous, bold, playful.

Now you have gilded everything except the cat (although you could gild its collar), the challenge is to find new directions, new beginnings, new projects. Attempting to recreate the look of gemstones and minerals like opal and lapis lazuli could be one of those projects. The lapis look can be created with veins of gold leaf or fine skewings of gold streaked across a background of peacock-blue distemper (Porter's). Try it.

Take on your world and enjoy recreating your environment. Live, learn and pass it on.

*Opposite, creating
lapis lazuli.*

Stencils

Here are stencil patterns used in this book. They can be enlarged, reversed or mirror-imaged.

A stencilled stool in a quiet corner. Seek out the other gilded pieces in the picture opposite.

Suppliers and distributors

Gilding Supplies

Australia:
WEYERMANN NOMINEES
PTY LTD
(Manufacturer and Distributor)
PO Box 912
Frankston
VIC 3199
Tel: 03 786 2247
Fax: 03 785 1145
(Mail order – catalogue on request)

New Zealand:
SIGNWRITERS SUPPLIES
35 Wilkinson Road
Ellerslie
Auckland
Tel: 09 525 6370
Fax:09 525 6373
(Mail order – catalogue on request)

USA:
SEPP LEAF PRODUCTS
381 Park Avenue South
New York NY 10016
Tel: (212) 683 2840
Fax: (212) 725 0308
(Mail order – catalogue on request)

Decals and Transfers

Australia:
THE DECAL SPECIALIST
PTY LTD
34 Balcombe Road
Mentone
VIC 3194
Tel: 03 585 0100
Fax: 03 585 0585
(Mail order – catalogue on request)

Gilding Kits

GILDING KITS AND CLASSES
Raebar Nominees
PO Box 388
Caulfield East
VIC 3145

Porter's Paints

HEAD OFFICE:
895 Bourke St
Waterloo
NSW 2017
Tel: 02 281 2413
(Mail order – catalogue on request)

MELBOURNE AGENT:
HARPER AND SANDILANDS
9 Almeida Crescent
South Yarra
VIC 3141
Tel: 03 826 3611
Fax: 03 826 2846
(Mail order – catalogue on request)

Decorative Arts Supplies
(including jaan, papier mâché, MDF, découpage)

ROMANTIQUE
HABERDASHERY
68 Milton Parade
Malvern
VIC 3144
(Contact June Wilhelm for gilding workshops)
Tel: 03 822 5293
Fax: 03 822 8577
(Mail order – catalogue on request)

Other products used in this book

PIONEER CRAFT
(Distributors for Deco Art and Ultra Gloss Enamel)
PO Box 403
Wahroonga
NSW 2076
Tel: 02 477 1239
Fax: 02 477 7357

INTERGRAIN PRODUCTS
(Manufacturers and distributors Australia wide)
1654 Centre Road
Springvale
VIC 3171
Tel: 03 558 4944
Fax: 03 558 4950
(Mail order – catalogue on request)

RIOT ART & CRAFT
PO Box 2328
North Brighton
VIC 3186
Tel: 03 882 8833
Fax: 03 596 2260
(Mail order – catalogue on request)

All of the above products can be found in retail outlets all over Australia.